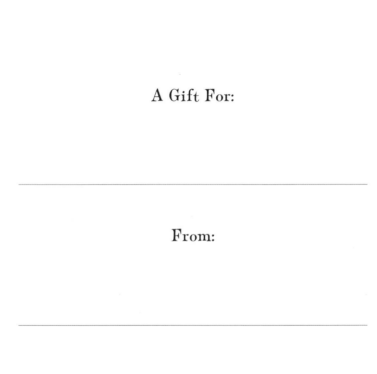

A Gift For:

_____

From:

_____

© 2006 Hallmark Licensing, Inc.
Visit us on the Web at www.Hallmark.com.

Art Direction: Kevin Swanson
Design & Illustration: Mary Eakin
Additional Illustration: Anita Colman
Production Artist: Dan C. Horton

Editorial Director: Todd Hafer
Editor: Jeff Morgan

Printed and bound in China.

ISBN: 1-59530-130-5

16 15 14 13 12 11 10 9 8 7

BOK4308

sisters

the best
(and sometimes most irritating)
of friends

written by Allyson E. Jones

The Jones sisters
as toddlers, teens,
and adults.

Introduction

My sister Stephanie, who is 15 months older than I am, was greatly annoyed when she realized I was here to stay. From the beginning, we competed for everything, and right through adolescence, we tried to drive each other bonkers. This is probably why I thought it was strange that my mom's best friend was her sister. I never saw them fight over the last cookie, much less take each other's favorite shoes without asking.

So imagine my surprise when I reached adulthood and realized I craved my sister's company. This person who had driven me crazy hogging the bathroom and changing the channel was now the friend I trusted the most.

Not only did my sister and I grow up to be best friends, but we even laugh about the things we once fought about. Well, most things. I'm still kind of mad about that sweater she took. She knows the one.

Allyson

Allyson E. Jones

The simple joys of childhood
are the best—
Popsicles®, swings,

footie

pajamas,

and getting your sister

in trouble.

There are so many stupid things to

double-dog

DARE

your sister to do,

and too few times
she can be talked into them.

Sisters share everything,

including *chicken pox*

and hot curlers.

All of your stuff also belongs to

your sister...

according
to her.

"Sister"

is just another word for "love,"

or, more specifically,

love to borrow.

A sister is someone

who doesn't just get you,

she also gets you in trouble.

She can turn you into a

giggling second-grader

in minutes...

he he he he he he he he he he

especially in church.

She's a friend who takes french fries

off your plate

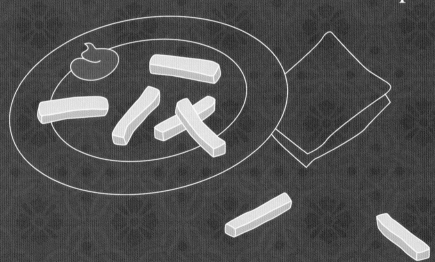

without asking.

She puts her own

unique stamp on the world.

In other words,
she has to have it *her way.*

Your sister is there
when you need her
and when you're

singing dramatically

into your hairbrush
   —and think you're alone.

She helps you get through
the break-out years.

She's also the one
pointing out the zits.

VOLC

NICE
ANO!

They share a
secret language

which consists mainly of

expressions and

rude gestures

when Mom isn't looking.

Things only
sisters
can say:

Let me fix your hair.

You're not
going out
with that guy.
Are you?

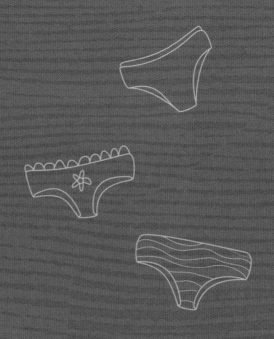

You need some
new underwear. ""

When you look into the mirror,
you see your sister
looking back at you...

because she is

hogging the mirror.

It is a well-known fact

that no *two sisters*

can enter a drugstore together

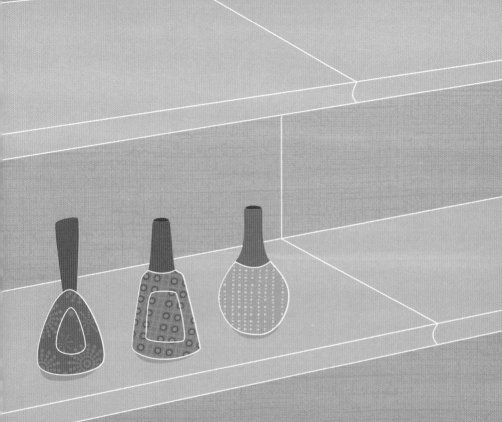

without spending some time
in the *makeup aisle.*

Making fun of your sister is

OFF-

LIMITS

to anyone else but you.

It's not hard to love
          and adore your sister.

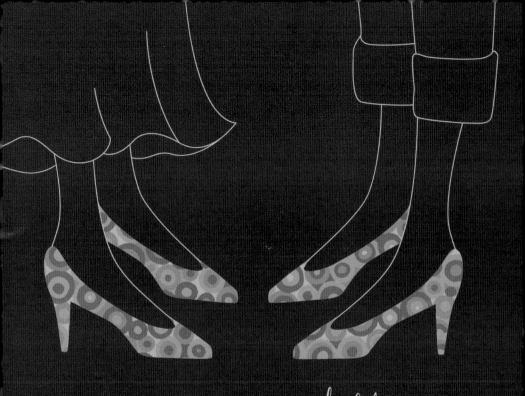

After all, she is *so much like you.*

Sisters always have someone to

roll their eyes with

at family gatherings.

The sister who
looks best in the picture
will have it up *on her fridge.*

Sisters are *always there*

when you're feeling bad.

Sometimes
they're the
cause.

They get through
stuff together:
challenges, difficulties, heartbreak,

cheesecakes, pizzas....

You can try to forget
all your *past boyfriends,*

but your sister probably won't let you.

Your sister will push you

to do *your best*—

slightly annoyed

perturbed

when she's not

pushing your buttons.

DO NOT PUSH!

She sees nothing even slightly odd about being your *harshest critic*

and also your *biggest supporter.*

Sisters are very encouraging.

In other words...

PY, SWEET, LOVING, CARIN

RETTY, HELPFUL, JOYFUL,

CE, GOOD-NATURED, PLAY

OPEFUL, GENUINE, KIND,

EAUTIFUL, KIND, GENEROU

NNY, SINCERE, HAPPY, LO

GREEABLE, LOVELY, OPTIM

BOSSY.

They're always willing

to give you advice...

whether you want it  or not.

They encourage you to
go for the best jobs.

After all, more income means

nicer birthday presents.

She helped make you
what you are today,

loyal and protective

of your jewelry.

(pop)

(rattle)

(clank)

A sister helps you
confront each obstacle
in your life.

Unless *it's her.*

Sisters can communicate
with very few words.

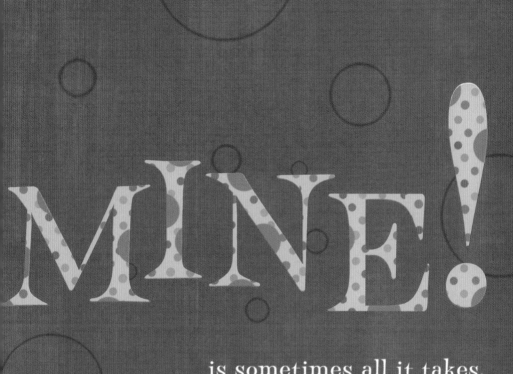

MINE!

is sometimes all it takes.

Your sister always knows
where to find you.

This is both comforting

and *mildly creepy.*

A sister is a friend you can adjust your

UNDERWEAR
in front of.

Sisters eventually stop competing
for their mom's attention

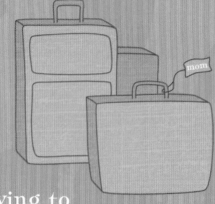

and start trying to *palm her off* on each other.

You trust
your sister
with the

most

precious

things

in your life...

any time you can get her to baby-sit.

Your sister is a *part of you.*
And she's not something
you can have removed

like an appendix.

Some stories are
only funny to one sister...

and she will tell them

over an

You will not be able to forget your

most embarrassing moments

as long as

your sister is alive.

A sister can make you laugh at stuff

you *thought you were mad* about.

How many times
does your sister have
to ask you if you rented
that movie she told you about

before you realize

it wasn't just a suggestion?

"All right already!"

Nothing fires up *sibling rivalry* like

adult sisters talking about
what they got for Christmas.

Even when someone

IRRITATES

the crap out of you,

you can still love her.

Sisters teach you that.

Life would be *so boring*
without your sister,

but you might actually get to finish . . . .
. . . .
. . . .

. . . .

. . . . .a sentence.

Something about
being with your sister and

drinking wine

can make you want to *sing in public*.

She is as precious as

Mom's diamond earrings,

which she thinks

she has dibs on.

Nothing bonds sisters

like the common goal of

not turning into

their mom.

Your sister helps you
cover up your *gray hairs,*

because she's the one who
found them in the first place.

When you look back on it,

it seems *silly that you fought*
with your sister so much.

She should have just accepted
that you were always right.

The best thing about
        having an older sister is
    when you're old,

        she's still older...

and the best thing
about having a younger sister
is that you'll always be more

mature and experienced.

About the Author

Allyson Jones was going to be a hairdresser but wound up writing funny Shoebox greeting cards for Hallmark instead. When she's not writing, she's busy watching her beloved television, dancing at concerts featuring forgotten 80s bands, and playing with her two cats—sisters named Cagney and Lacey. She does have an actual sister named Stephanie with whom she shares the kind of close, affectionate, sometimes annoying relationship that qualifies her to write this book. Like her writing, Allyson is wickedly funny, honest, sweet, warm, and sassy. She has more friends than anybody, and they all wish they had sisters just like her.

If you've enjoyed this book,

we'd love to hear from you.

Book Feedback
2501 McGee, Mail Drop 215
Kansas City, MO 64141-6580

Or e-mail us at:
booknotes@hallmark.com